W9-ASD-479

THE LIPIZZAN HORSE

By Sara Green

Consultant:
Dr. Emily Leuthner
DVM, MS, DACVIM
Country View Veterinary Service
Oregon, Wisc.

BELLWETHER MEDIA • MINNEAPOLIS, MN

Jump into the cockpit and take flight with Pilot Books. Your journey will take you on high-energy adventures as you learn about all that is wild, weird, fascinating, and fun!

This edition first published in 2012 by Bellwether Media, Inc.

No part of this publication may be reproduced in whole or in part without written permission of the publisher. For information regarding permission, write to Bellwether Media, Inc., Attention: Permissions Department, 5357 Penn Avenue South, Minneapolis, MN 55419.

Library of Congress Cataloging-in-Publication Data

Green, Sara, 1964-
The Lipizzan horse / by Sara Green.
    p. cm. – (Pilot books. horse breed roundup)
Includes bibliographical references and index.
Summary: "Engaging images accompany information about the Lipizzan Horse. The combination of high-interest subject matter and narrative text is intended for students in grades 3 through 7"–Provided by publisher.
ISBN 978-1-60014-738-8 (hardcover : alk. paper)
1. Lipizzaner horse–Juvenile literature. 1. Title.
SF293.L5G74 2012
636.1'38–dc23   2011028866

Printed in the United States of America, North Mankato, MN.

010112   1204

CONTENTS

The Lipizzan Horse

Music fills the air while thousands await the majestic performance. As the music swells, twelve white horses and their costumed riders enter the arena. The riders sit straight and tall, confidently guiding the horses with small movements. The horse ballet has begun! For the next two hours, magnificent Lipizzan horses will march, leap, jump, and kick to classical and modern music. It is no wonder people call Lipizzans "the dancing white stallions."

The Lipizzan, called the Lipizzaner in Europe, is an elegant, intelligent horse with a friendly **temperament**. Lipizzans are shorter than many other breeds. They stand between 14 and 16 **hands** tall at the **withers**. They usually weigh between 1,000 and 1,300 pounds (450 and 590 kilograms).

Lipizzans have a very distinct appearance. They are a strong, sturdy breed with compact bodies, strong backs, thick necks, and wide **girths**. Powerful **hindquarters** allow Lipizzans to stand up on their back legs and perform difficult moves. Their short, perky ears lie on each side of a long, silky mane. Their noses curve out slightly just below their dark, expressive eyes.

Lipizzans are known for their bright white coats. However, Lipizzan **foals** are born with brown, dark gray, or black coats. Their coats turn white as they grow. When Lipizzans are between 6 and 10 years old, their coats become all white.

7

Royal Horses, Daring Rescues

The Lipizzan breed began over 400 years ago in Europe. In 1580, Archduke Charles II started a breeding farm. It was in the small town of Lipizza, an area that is now part of Slovenia. The Archduke wanted strong, **agile** warhorses. He bred horses from the Karst region of Slovenia with Andalusian horses from Spain. The Karst horses were small, strong, and white. The Andalusians were elegant, brave warhorses. The results of this **crossbreeding** were high-stepping, hardy white horses. Over time, the horses born on this farm came to be known as Lipizzaners, or Lipizzans. Only Austrian royalty and military leaders were allowed to ride them.

In the late 1700s and early 1800s, breeders brought six new **stallions** to Lipizza to breed with the Lipizzans. Later, two more stallions started separate breeding lines in Hungary and Croatia. These eight stallions became the **foundation horses** for the modern breed.

The Foundation Stallions

Pluto—a gray Spanish stallion, born in 1765

Conversano—a black Neapolitan stallion, born in 1767

Favory—a dun stallion, born in 1779

Neapolitano—a bay Neapolitan stallion, born in 1790

Incitato—a Hungarian stallion, born in 1802

Siglavy—a gray Arabian stallion, born in 1810

Maestoso—a gray Spanish stallion, born in 1819

Tulipan—a Spanish stallion, born in the late 1800s

In addition, there are around 35 recognized mare lines. The first one was established in 1776.

The history of the Lipizzan is closely tied to the Spanish Riding School in Vienna, Austria. Planning for the school began in the late 1500s. It wasn't until a few hundred years later that the school began to train the first Lipizzans and riders in the art of **classical dressage**. Thousands of Lipizzans have attended the school.

Spanish Riding School

Alois Podhajsky

General George Patton

Lipizzans faced terrible threats during World War II. At this time, most Lipizzan stallions lived in Austria at the Spanish Riding School. Alois Podhajsky was the director of the school. He feared the war was getting too close. He sent the stallions to St. Martin, Austria, where they would be safe. However, the **mares** and foals were in Hostau, Czechoslovakia. Battles raged all around them. In 1945, United States Army General George Patton sent a unit of American soldiers to move the mares and foals. They took them to Wels, Austria. The heroic actions of these two men saved the breed.

Family Name

Both stallions and mares are named in traditional ways. The name of a registered Lipizzan stallion has two parts. One part comes from his father, or sire. The other part comes from his mother, or dam. A mare is named after an ancestor on her dam's side.

The first Lipizzans came to the United States in 1937. The Austrian government gave them as gifts to opera singer Countess Maria Jeritza. In 1958, Tempel Smith brought 14 Lipizzan mares and 6 stallions to the U.S. Over time, more Lipizzans arrived in the United States. American Lipizzan owners eventually decided to create a **registry** to keep track of **pedigrees**. They formed the Lipizzan Association of America (LAA) in 1969. In 1992, the LAA changed its name to the Lipizzan Association of North America (LANA). A second American registry called the United States Lipizzan Registry (USLR) formed in 1980.

A Lipizzan must have a pedigree that traces back to foundation stallions or mares to be registered with either the LANA or the USLR. Together, these registeries have between 1,100 and 1,500 registered Lipizzans. An additional 2,000 Lipizzans are registered in other countries. With fewer than 4,000 Lipizzans in the world today, the breed remains rare.

The Elegant, Dancing Lipizzans

For hundreds of years, Lipizzans have been bred to perform the elegant moves of classical dressage. This style of horse training and riding is based on techniques developed long ago by the Greeks. In classical dressage, trainers move in subtle ways to guide Lipizzans through a variety of movements. Horses first learn simple **gaits** and turns. As their skills improve, they learn complex footwork and **choreography**.

One of the highlights of a Lipizzan dressage performance is the Quadrille. In the Quadrille, four, six, or eight Lipizzans and their riders perform an intricate dance together. The horses move in **unison** to create a variety of complex **formations** while music plays. One of the most difficult moves is called the half-pass. In a half-pass, horses move forward and sideways at the same time.

A spectacular part of a Lipizzan classical dressage performance is the **Airs Above the Ground**. The Lipizzan is one of only a few breeds to do the Airs. Only the most talented Lipizzans are able to learn them. The Airs are complex leaps, jumps, and moves performed in the air. The Airs were originally intended for use in ancient battles. Soldiers on horseback guided horses to do these movements to protect themselves and intimidate their enemies. Today's Lipizzans perform the Airs to entertain audiences around the world.

The Airs Above the Ground

Capriole
A difficult leap into the air. At the height of the leap, the horse kicks out dramatically with its hind legs.

Levade
The horse balances on its haunches, maintaining an angle of 45 degrees or less to the ground for a short period of time.

Courbette
The horse balances on its hind legs and then hops forward, keeping its hind legs together and front legs off the ground.

Mezair
The horse sits in a levade position and kicks out with its front legs.

capriole

Famous Lipizzans

"World Famous" Lipizzaner Stallions

The "World Famous" Lipizzaner Stallions are a group of 12 to 14 Lipizzans that perform classical dressage around the world. Riders wear costumes that represent different periods in history. The majority of the stallions come from Austria. Since 1970, more than 23 million people have attended their performances.

Maestoso II Sabrina

Maestoso II Sabrina, also called Smokey, was a champion stallion born in 1976 at Tempel Farms in Illinois. In 1989, Smokey won the United States Dressage Federation Horse of the Year award. He fathered more than 95 foals, many of which became classical dressage champions.

Pluto Bona II

Pluto Bona II, known as Beau, was a classical dressage champion. He became one of the most important breeding Lipizzans in the United States in the late 1900s. When Beau was 17 years old, he earned the title of Champion Stallion at the first Lipizzan show held in the United States.

"World Famous"
Lipizzaner Stallions

19

Lipizzans also participate in activities outside of the **show ring**. Older Lipizzans make great riding horses for people of all ages. Young Lipizzans are often too energetic for beginning riders. Lipizzans also pull carriages. Many tourists visit Lipizza for carriage rides on the grounds where the breed began.

People admire Lipizzans for many reasons. The breed is beautiful, talented, and rare. It has faced several challenges in its history and managed to survive. Now Lipizzans charm audiences around the world with their exceptional strength, discipline, and grace. No one can resist the striking presence of a magnificent Lipizzan!

Glossary

agile—able to move the body quickly and with ease

Airs Above the Ground—a series of classical dressage movements in which horses lift their front hooves or their bodies off the ground

choreography—a planned sequence of steps and moves

classical dressage—a method of training horses to perform moves developed by the ancient Greeks; it emphasizes riding in harmony with the horse.

crossbreeding—using two different breeds of an animal to produce a new breed

foals—young horses; foals are under one year old.

formations—arrangements of groups into specific patterns

foundation horses—the first horses of a specific breed; all other horses of the breed can trace their bloodlines back to foundation horses.

gaits—the ways in which a horse moves; walking, trotting, and cantering are examples of gaits.

girths—distances around the bellies of animals

hands—the units used to measure the height of a horse; one hand is equal to 4 inches (10.2 centimeters).

hindquarters—the hind legs and muscles of a four-legged animal

mares—adult female horses

pedigrees—records or lists of ancestors

registry—a collection of the births, names, and pedigrees of horses of the same breed; owners register their horses with a registry.

show ring—the ring where horses compete and are displayed at a horse show

stallions—adult male horses that are used for breeding

temperament—personality or nature; the Lipizzan has an intelligent, friendly temperament.

unison—at the same time

withers—the ridge between the shoulder blades of a horse

At the Library

Funston, Sylvia. *The Kids' Horse Book*. Toronto, Ont.: Maple Tree Press, 2004.

Saunders, Susan. *Riding School Rivals: The Story of a Majestic Lipizzan Horse and the Girls Who Fight for the Right to Ride Him*. Dyersville, Iowa: Ertl Co., 1996.

Stone, Lynn M. *Lipizzans*. Vero Beach, Fla.: Rourke Corp., 1998.

On the Web

Learning more about Lipizzans is as easy as 1, 2, 3.

1. Go to www.factsurfer.com.

2. Enter "Lipizzans" into the search box.

3. Click the "Surf" button and you will see a list of related Web sites.

With factsurfer.com, finding more information is just a click away.

Index

The images in this book are reproduced through the courtesy of: Juniors Bildarchiv / Age Fotostock, front cover, pp. 6-7, 12-13; Dr. Ajay Kumar Singh, pp. 4-5, 8-9, 19; Hanz Punz/ Associated Press, pp. 10, 14-15; PhotoQuest / Getty Images, p. 11; Roland Schlager / epa / Corbis, pp. 16-17; Juniors Bildarchiv / Photolibrary, pp. 20-21.